The Mona Lisa Caper

RICK JACOBSON

Illustrated by

LAURA FERNANDEZ & RICK JACOBSON

TUNDRA BOOKS

Published in Canada by Tundra Books,
481 University Avenue, Toronto, Ontario M5G 2E9

Published in the United States by Tundra Books of Northern New York,
P.O. Box 1030, Plattsburgh, New York 12901

Library of Congress Control Number: 2004098877

Library and Archives Canada Cataloguing in Publication

Jacobson, Rick
     The Mona Lisa caper / Rick Jacobson ; illustrated by Laura
Fernandez
and Rick Jacobson.

ISBN 0-88776-726-5

     I. Fernandez, Laura II. Title.

PS8619.A26M66 2005   C813'.6   C2004-906555-6

We acknowledge the financial support of the Government of Canada through the Book
Publishing Industry Development Program (BPIDP) and that of the Government of
Ontario through the Ontario Media Development Corporation's Ontario Book Initiative.
We further acknowledge the support of the Canada Council for the Arts and the Ontario
Arts Council for our publishing program.

The quote on the facing page is taken from *The Ingenious Gentleman Don Quixote
de la Mancha,* by Miguel de Cervantes.

Mona Lisa by Leonardo da Vinci reproduced with permission of: Réunion des
Musées Nationaux/Art Resource, NY

The illustrations for this book were rendered in watercolor on BKF Rives printmaking paper.

Design: Kong Njo

Printed in Hong Kong, China

1 2 3 4 5 6   10 09 08 07 06 05

And so, to sum it all up,
I perceive everything I say as absolutely true,
and deficient in nothing whatever,
and paint it all in my mind
exactly as I want it to be.

– DON QUIXOTE

THANK YOU TO:

Mark Weinstock,
Jeff Bessner,
Chris Clapperton,
and Mor.

Hanging on a wall year after year is not as easy as you might think. In fact, it's tiring, and I often wish I could take a holiday. Once, very long ago, I did just that. Of course, I had quite a bit of help.

It was 1911, and the world famous Louvre Museum in Paris was in an uproar. Many of its treasures, including me, were being photographed so that the museum staff could keep track of us all. At the same time, workers were hired to make display cases for many of the paintings. One of those workers became a friend of mine. His name was Vincenzo Perugia.

Vincenzo built the box that now held me safe. Every day at noon, he sat before me, eating his sandwich and speaking in Italian. At first I found it hard to understand him. You see, although I had been painted in Italy by the great genius, Leonardo da Vinci, I hadn't heard the language spoken for a long time. Little by little I began to understand everything he said. He talked about Italy and how homesick he was, and as he spoke,

a strange feeling came over me. I realized that I missed my country too. I missed the fresh air and the smells and the people in the streets. Though I tried to tell Vincenzo, he couldn't hear me.

Then one day, with his mouth still full of his last bite, he said something that surprised me.

"I think you miss Italy as much as I."

After a short pause, Vincenzo went back to work.

Early in the morning a few days later, Vincenzo came and took me down from the wall. I was very excited. I was also frightened!

My friend wrapped me in a big cloth and tied it firmly. As luck would have it, there was a small hole near my right eye and I could see out.

Vincenzo carried me through galleries and down stairs. He ran into a little trouble when he came to a locked side door, but someone came along and taking no notice of me, helped as Vincenzo removed the doorknob. Vincenzo slipped the doorknob into his pocket, thanked the man, and left the Louvre — just like that. It was the first time I had been outside in over a hundred years. It was wonderful!

Up until now, I had never really seen the city. Paris was beautiful, especially in the morning light as the sun rose higher and cast a warm glow over everything. Vincenzo walked quickly, pausing only to toss the doorknob from his pocket as we wound through twisting alleys toward his home.

He lived in a small third-floor flat. Each morning before Vincenzo headed off to work, he would slip me under his bed and I would simply listen. When he returned, he would bring me out, remove my cloth, and set me on a chair a short distance from a window. I could see the Paris skyline with its twinkling lights and hear outside noises. Vincenzo would talk about everything – his home in Italy and his work.

And so it continued. During the day, I remained under the bed and listened to everyone who lived in and around the building. I grew to know shopkeepers, bankers, mothers, and children by their voices. At night from my chair, I enjoyed Vincenzo's stories and the magic of Paris nights. I couldn't imagine being happier, but then, I didn't know what was in store for me.

At first Vincenzo was nervous. He told me the museum was crawling with gendarmes and inspectors, all looking for me. He was afraid they would discover that he was the one who had taken me from the Louvre. In fact, they did question him, but they let him go. He read me newspaper stories about the kidnapping, and he told me what he had heard about the investigation.

I listened to the talk on the street. People were very upset. They missed me and I felt guilty for enjoying my freedom. If only I could tell Vincenzo, but my lips were painted firmly in place. They smiled, but would not form words.

One morning Vincenzo did not go to work. He went out and didn't return until dusk. He took me out from under the bed, but did not unwrap me or put me on my chair. Instead, he set me by the door, muttering that it was time for us to leave. Someone had found the doorknob. The French police were asking too many questions. Vincenzo and I were going to escape to our homeland!

W hen Vincenzo was ready, he picked me up and headed for the street. It was late October and it was raining – not hard, but I could feel it in the air. Vincenzo tenderly placed me on the back seat of his little car and drove away. As we left, I thought about the neighbors I would never see or hear again.

The ride through Paris was long and the noises and smells kept changing. Vincenzo seemed tense and pushed the little car through traffic, often blasting the horn, only to be answered by other horns. I was happy when the city sounds were eventually replaced by the *pssssh* of our tires on wet country roads.

Gradually Vincenzo relaxed and began to talk to me. At first he spoke only about what we were passing, but as his tension eased, he described Italy for me. No vehicles had passed us for some time when Vincenzo slowed the car. The sound of the tires changed as they left the pavement, crunched on gravel, then stopped on a deserted side road. Vincenzo turned the engine off, shifted in his seat, and within minutes I heard his familiar deep breathing. He was asleep.

Hour after hour I listened to the night noises of small creatures. Their quiet rustlings gradually gave way to a chorus of birdsong as the sun rose.

Vincenzo woke with a big stretch, and within minutes we were on our way again. The road was dry today and the little car seemed livelier. Vincenzo burst into song. Still covered on the back seat, I listened. The traffic was light and the road, although curvy, was smooth. The sun shone through the window and warmed me in a faintly familiar way. It was delicious.

Vincenzo rolled down the window and I could smell the sweet scent

of grass, wet with morning dew. Cuckoos called over the purr of the car's engine. A playful gust of wind loosened my wrapping and suddenly I could see. My eyes filled with the warm yellow light of a glorious day. We rushed past trees and I recognized them. They mirrored the ones painted behind me. I was back in the land where I had been created! It was beautiful – so full of color, sound, and fragrance. Those precious few hours on that road were the happiest in all my five hundred years.

By early evening, Florence lay before us. We had come over a low hill and Vincenzo announced, "We're home."

He reached behind and pulled my covering back into place. I was able to catch only a quick glimpse of the magnificent dome and marble towers at the city's center, the criss-cross of bridges, and the ribbon of river, shimmering gold in the sunset. Still, I recognized everything. This could only be Florence.

Vincenzo rented a small room at the Hotel Tripoli, and just as in Paris, the window opened onto the world I had missed for many years.

We settled into our familiar routine. Every day I listened under the bed and every evening I watched Florence from my window. We were happy for several months. Then one evening I heard unfamiliar voices in our room.

Vincenzo and I were not alone!

I was brought out from under the bed and my wrapping was removed. Two strangers stood before me with shocked expressions on their faces. One leaned forward and peered at me for a closer look. I soon learned that he was an art dealer named Alfredo Geri. His friend was Giovanne Poggie. I didn't like them, and I certainly didn't trust them.

Vincenzo rambled on about Italy and the rights of the people and many other things I didn't really understand. As the two men examined me, they exchanged secret glances. Something was terribly wrong and Vincenzo didn't seem to notice. I tried to warn him, to catch his attention, but once more, my words were sealed in the paint and Vincenzo couldn't hear me.

And then, to my horror, I realized that Vincenzo had sold me! Alfredo tied my covering around me, but just before I was wrapped in darkness, my eyes met Vincenzo's. There was the deep sadness of goodbye in them. Without words, I said goodbye too. Our great adventure was over. I never saw Vincenzo again.

Once more, I was taken through the streets of Florence, but there was no enjoyment this time. I could only wonder what Vincenzo would do; where he would go now. When my cover was finally lifted, I was back in the still air of a museum. Again, people seemed surprised to see me. They examined me, compared me to photographs, scrutinized my brush strokes, and even inspected the cracks in my varnish. With great satisfaction they wisely concluded I was who I had been all along – Leonardo da Vinci's *Mona Lisa*.

A uniformed detective arrived and spoke with Alfredo and Giovanne. They told him how they had bought me and called the authorities, realizing I was the painting everyone was looking for. And they talked about my friend. When the detective left, I knew Vincenzo was in serious trouble.

Before my return to the Louvre I toured Italy, visiting museums in Florence, Milan, and Rome. I didn't mind being back. Not really. People were so happy to see me and more than once I overheard them talking about Vincenzo. He had been arrested, of course, and put on trial. After that he was released. I thought he might come to see me, but I suppose that he could not.

If *you* ever come to visit and notice me smiling my own private little smile, you will know it's because I'm lost in pleasant thoughts, remembering a holiday – remembering a friend.

Leonardo da Vinci painted the *Mona Lisa* between 1503 and 1506. Although it is not shown to scale for this story, the actual portrait is quite small – 53 cm X 77 cm (20 7/8″ X 30″) – and was painted in oils on a poplar wood panel. For five hundred years, people have been fascintated by the lady with the smile. In Italy she is called *La Gioconda*. In France she is known as *La Jaconde*. Both terms mean "the lighthearted woman" and they refer to the name of the lady who sat for the picture. Lisa Gherardini Giocondo would likely have smiled more broadly had she known how many people would eventually come to see her face and how widely traveled her portrait would be.

The Men Who Loved Her

The Mona Lisa Caper is based on true events that began to unfold on Monday, August 21, 1911. On that day, Vincenzo Perugia shocked the world by stealing the most famous of the many treasured paintings in the Louvre.

Though Vincenzo was a thief, he meant well. He simply wanted to return the painting to the Italian people in the mistaken belief that it had been stolen from them. Unfortunately for him, the rightful owners disagreed, and the law was on their side.

Vincenzo was arrested, and at his trial the press had a field day. Vincenzo won the hearts of Italians with his patriotism and frequent outbursts. In fact, he received so much food, wine, clothing, and furniture that he had to be moved to a larger cell. He even had offers of marriage! The jury found him guilty as charged, but his seven-month sentence had already been served by the time his lengthy trial ended, and so he was released. He had become something of a hero in Italy.

Leonardo da Vinci was the amazing genius who created the *Mona Lisa* during the Renaissance – a period of intense artistic activity in Italy. Painter, inventor, scientist, architect, and visionary, Leonardo completed great masterpieces in his time, but this little portrait was said to be his personal favorite. The lady with the secretive smile has inspired mystery, intrigue, rumor, and music in her five-hundred-year lifetime. Da Vinci's misty way of painting, a technique he developed and called *sfumato,* is very atmospheric and has much to do with the spell *Mona Lisa* casts on her viewers. It is thought that Leonardo sold the painting to King François I of France, long before Vincenzo was fascinated by her. That is most likely how she came to be in Paris. After touring Italy, the *Mona Lisa* was returned to the Louvre where she remains to this day. Though millions have visited her since, Vincenzo Perugia never saw her again. A hundred years later, the *Mona Lisa* is still smiling.